GREAT PICTURES

AND THEIR STORIES

How To Look At Pictures

"You must look at pictures studiously, earnestly, honestly. It will take years before you come to a full appreciation of art; but when at last you have it, you will be possessed of the purest, loftiest and most ennobling pleasures that the civilized world can offer you."

JOHN C. VAN DYKE.

ST.
AA
PRESS

GREAT PICTURES
AND THEIR STORIES

INTERPRETING
MASTERPIECES
TO CHILDREN

BY
KATHERINE MORRIS LESTER

BOOK FOUR

This book was originally published in 1927
by Mentzer, Bush & Company.

This facsimile edition reprinted in 2024
with improved color images
by St. Augustine Academy Press.

ISBN: 978-1-64051-147-7

CONTENTS

INDEX OF ILLUSTRATIONS IN GREAT PICTURES AND THEIR STORIES

FOREWORD

Picture Study is rapidly becoming an important factor in our public school education. "Nearly every progressive city," says the Bureau of Education, Washington, D. C., "is making use of some form of picture study in the public school system."

The twentieth century has ushered in the reproduction of masterpieces in colors! To what heights of delight the children of the public schools may be carried by the famous pictures of the world in color!

It remains only for the elders to choose pictures adapted to the childish interests; pictures which will cultivate a taste for the best in art; pictures which through the impressionable early years will lead to a true understanding and appreciation of the world's masterpieces!

In preparing this series of readers it has been the aim of those selecting the pictures to consider always the child interest. The field of pictures is large. Not only have the "old masters" been drawn upon, but masters in modern art as well, including modern American artists. Thus constantly, through this series of pictures, the principles of beauty which made possible the "old masters" of yesterday are seen again in the art of today.

In the preparation of the text the child's interest and his ability to read are carefully considered. Real picture knowledge is conveyed in the child's own language.

In the primary grades the interest is largely in "what it is all about." Consequently the text aims to satisfy this curiosity, and at the same time lead to unconscious observation of those things which are most alive to the little child,—color, life, action.

The vocabulary for Books I, II, and III is based on "The Reading Vocabulary," * the Horn, Horn, and Packer List.

*See twenty-fourth Year Book, National Society for the Study of Education, Part I, 1925.

In the intermediate grades, a lively interest in the story is always uppermost. Gradually an appreciation of picture-pattern develops. Simple elements in picture making,—i.e. center of interest, repetition of line and color,—may be intelligently comprehended by children of the intermediate grades.

In the grammar grades great interest in the story continues, and with this interest there develops an appreciation of HOW the story is told,—the real ART of the picture. The pupil not only learns that the picture is a masterpiece, but WHY. He thus acquires standards for judging other pictures.

Each picture is followed by a short sketch of the artist, told in a key adapted to the age and interest of the pupil.

The questions which follow the text will assist in developing an intelligent appreciation of the picture.

The author is particularly indebted to Miss Jennie Long, recently Supervisor of Primary

Education, Peoria Public Schools, for valuable criticism of the primary text. Grateful acknowledgment is also made for the opportunity of practical work with a selected number of primary stories in the schools of Peoria.

The manuscripts of the intermediate and grammar grade books have been submitted to teachers of these grades, to whom the author is indebted for helpful practical suggestions.

The MUSICAL SELECTIONS for the pictures have been graciously contributed by Eva G. Kidder, Director of Music, Peoria Public Schools. The author believes this to be a very valuable feature of these books.

KATHERINE MORRIS LESTER.

ILLUSTRATED WITH REPRO-
DUCTIONS IN COLOR FROM
THE ORIGINAL MASTER-
PIECES, BY COURTESY OF
THE ART EXTENSION
SOCIETY OF NEW YORK.

THE AURORA

Rospigliosi Palace, Rome

ARTIST: Guido Reni
SCHOOL: Italian
DATES: 1575-1642

AURORA

Good morning, good morning, good morning to you!

A beautiful day is dawning!

A joyous day of golden sunshine and blue skies will soon be here. Apollo, the driver of the sun-chariot, urges his fiery steeds up, up, and up over the clouds of night. He brings with him the new day.

See the sleeping world! It is far, far below. All is dark and still. The clouds are just beginning to roll away.

See Apollo in his golden chariot! He holds in one hand the reins of his fiery steeds! With flying manes and gleaming eyes, they are eager to be off.

Have you ever seen the first rosy

light of morning? This faint, rosy light tells that the day is on its way. We call it "dawn."

The artist, in his picture, placed "Dawn" going before the horses of Apollo. Her real name is "Aurora." She is Goddess of the Dawn. She is a beautiful rosy light. She says to the sleeping world, "Wake! Wake! the day has come!" She scatters flowers over the sleeping earth.

Ah! And do you see the bright morning star?

The bright morning star is the last star to be seen before the sun arrives. Yes! There he is, just behind Aurora. He carries a flaming torch.

But he, too, will disappear when the sun comes up. It will not be long. The golden chariot wheel will edge up over the horizon. Its ruddy glow will fall upon the waking world. Then the new day with its many hours begins. Hours to sing. Hours to dance. Hours to play. Hours to work. So many hours make a day!

Apollo, the sun god, knows all about the day, so he brings the hours with him. There they come, dancing about the chariot. One, two, three, four, five, six, seven. Seven hours. Hand in hand they come, dancing merrily around the golden sun of day.

How light they seem as they glide along, their feet scarcely resting upon the clouds! These must be the light morning hours, they seem so joyous and free. Perhaps there are hours that we cannot see on the other side of the chariot. Yes, perhaps over there are the late afternoon hours.

See the bright colors! The artist wanted to tell of the light and joy of the new day, so he used gay yellow and orange, and blue, green, and violet. The bright colors and the happy swinging hours make beautiful music as the day comes on.

By and by the chariot will reach the highest point in the heavens. Then it will be midday. Later, as the sun slowly sinks to rest, we know that Apollo is completing his journey. When he disappears over the western horizon, the earth will be in slumber. By and by, after twelve long hours, another day will dawn. Again Apollo and his happy dancing hours will lead the way for the next new day.

The story of Apollo is very, very old. Over three hundred years ago, one of the greatest artists of Italy painted this story of Apollo and the Hours upon the ceiling of a fine old palace in Rome. There it has remained to this day.

The ceilings in these old palaces were so very high that the workers had to build great scaffolds in order to reach them. Upon a high scaffold, the artist collected all his materials. There, lying flat upon his back, or crouching in a low position, he worked day after day, and week after week.

Sometimes it was a year and more before these wonderful ceiling pictures were finished.

Our picture, "Aurora," is so very high that it is difficult to study it from below. To make it more comfortable and easy for visitors, a table, with a large mirror placed flat upon it, has been set in the hall. It is set in such a way that the painting upon the ceiling is reflected in the mirror below. Thus, the picture may be easily studied.

Today travelers from all over the world are constantly visiting the palace. There one may see them, seated about the table, studying the picture by looking into the mirror instead of up to the ceiling, which would be quite difficult.

THE ARTIST

The artist, Guido Reni, was the son of a musician and singer of Italy. The father taught his son to sing and play on the flute and harpsichord. He intended that he should grow up and become a singer and musician like himself.

The little Guido, however, liked best to draw, and paint, and model in clay. He used to run away from his music lessons and go to a near by studio. Here he could work with the paints and clay as much as he liked.

After the lad was older and had made some progress in his drawing, his work was observed by a well known painter. The artist recognized the boy's talent, and advised his father to send him to a teacher. The father consented, but added,— "If Guido doesn't do well at painting, he must go back to his music."

Much to his father's delight, however, the boy made great progress. It was just about this time that the little artist grew to be very beautiful. Indeed, so beautiful did he become that many of the older artists were eager to paint his picture. One of the famous painters of the day painted him as an angel in several of his pictures.

By the time he was thirteen, he was so skillful in the use of the pencil and brush that his teacher allowed him to instruct the other pupils.

The pupils loved their little teacher. They listened to all he said. They liked to watch him take a pencil or brush and sketch a picture.

It was not long before the fame of the youthful Guido spread to the great cities of Italy. Many honors came to him. By and by he was called upon to decorate one of the princely palaces of Rome.

There upon the ceiling of the great hall of the palace he painted the famous "Aurora."

For over three hundred years, travelers have been going to Italy to see this great picture painted so long ago. Today it is one of the twelve great pictures of the world, truly a great masterpiece!

Though Guido Reni grew to be one of the world's celebrated painters, he never entirely forgot his music. We see his love for music in the beautiful dancing Hours of his "Aurora."

DIRECTED STUDY

1. What story does the picture tell?

2. Who is the sun-god?
   What does he do?
   What kind of a chariot
      does he drive?

3. Who is Aurora?
   What does she do?
   Where is the morning star?
   What does he do?

4. When will the day begin?
   What are the dancing figures?
   What makes joy in the picture?
   What makes music in the picture?

5. How does the artist tell of the
       joy of the new day?
   How does he tell of the quiet-
       ness of the sleeping world?
   How does he tell that
       Apollo is the sun-god?

6. Who is the artist?
   Where did he paint this picture?
   When did he paint it?
   Do you like it? Why?

Related Music: MORNING .... *Grieg*
                JOY OF MORNING.*Ware*

THE HORSE FAIR
Metropolitan Museum, New York

ARTIST: Rosa Bonheur
SCHOOL: French
DATES: 1822-1899

THE HORSE FAIR

What a proud, prancing procession of fine horses!

They are on the way to the Paris fair. Here their keepers will lead them up and down the great parade, showing off their strength and beauty to the very best advantage. Perhaps many may be sold. Perhaps a grand prize may be given to the finest. How proudly they sweep by!

The dapple-gray Percherons are very conscious of their beauty. See their glossy coats and gracefully arched necks!

Just back of them is a rearing black colt. Possibly he is from Arabia. Beside him is a white colt. He follows the example of the black one by plunging and rearing about playfully.

Trotting along beside them is a quiet little pony with a blanket strapped to his back. He, perhaps is not to be sold. He may carry one of the keepers back to the country.

What a fine black steed comes trotting up at the left! His head is up. His mane and tail fly to the breeze. With even pace his keeper trots along beside him. They have had a spirited run on this broad highway shaded with trees. Away into the hazy distance march the trees! They make a fine background for the moving forms of the horses. On they come! On they come, this proud, prancing parade!

Each horse has a groom. One man, however, drives the two powerful draft horses. It takes all his strength to control this spirited team. He leans far back as he holds the reins. His rolled up sleeve shows the muscular arm, and his firm grip on the rein.

There are many more horses in the picture than we see at first. Some one has counted thirty. The artist, however, wanted us to see a few distinctly, so she painted the more important ones very carefully. She chose the beautiful dapple-grays and blacks because they make a fine contrast of dark and light. She painted the sun falling full upon the powerful grays, making them the most important in the picture. Next we see the rearing black and white, and then the fine black steed bringing up the rear.

Notice the patches of shadow on the ground. Can you tell where the sun is?

Can you tell the time of day?

On they go to the open spaces beyond! The fluttering blouse of the foremost rider and the scampering feet of his horse lead the way.

Many of the people in the picture are beyond the trees. Here is the market-place with its track. Here the crowd is waiting for the on-coming parade.

For a long time, people did not believe that the picture had been painted by a woman. Because it was so large, and the animals so powerful, they thought that it could have been painted only by a man. The French woman, however, Rosa Bonheur, is the greatest animal painter of the world.

THE ARTIST

All her life long Rosa Bonheur loved to draw and paint animals. Cattle, horses, donkeys, lions, and other four-footed creatures were her delight.

Rosa was the oldest of four children. All of these children could draw, and model in clay. Rosa could draw before she could write. She attended school with other children, but the margins of her books were covered with sketches of all kinds of animals.

Rosa's father was a painter, and taught the little girl much about drawing and painting. Though he knew she had much talent, he decided that she must learn to be a dressmaker. So Rosa went to learn the dressmaking trade.

By and by, however, the father marvelled at her wonderful drawings; for though she was learning to sew she still kept on with her sketches. Then he changed his mind. He now said: "Rosa must learn to draw and paint." So the little artist gave up the dressmaking trade and gave all her time to art study.

She walked through the streets of Paris and out through the country, studying the animals she saw.

By and by she became known as the "animal painter" of France. She painted many celebrated pictures of oxen, cows, horses, and dogs. Before painting our picture,—"The Horse Fair,"—she made a study of horses in all positions. She drew them rearing, tossing their heads, running, trotting, and galloping. A woman artist was not permitted to go freely among the horses; so Rosa Bonheur cut off her hair and wore men's clothes, so she would not be noticed as she studied at the horse stalls.

She was eager for her native village to buy her picture, and offered it for $2400. The village, however, did not buy. Instead an English firm purchased it for $8000. In 1887 it was sold to an American for $55,000. The buyer presented it to the Metropolitan Museum of New York City, where it now hangs.

The artist once said: "I love to catch the rapid motion of animals, and the light and color in their glossy coats."

In this great picture we see the rapid
motion and the shiny coats she loved
to paint.

DIRECTED STUDY

1. Where are the horses going?
   Do they want to go?
   Why do you think so?

2. Do you see all the horses dis-
      tinctly?
   Which do you see first?
   Which do you see next? Next?
   Why do you see them in this
      order?

3. Which horses seem proud? Meek?
      Frightened? Spirited?
   Which do you like best?

4. Where is the sun? How do you know?

   Where is the "center of interest"?

   How is it emphasized?

5. Which is more interesting,—the horses or the landscape? Why?

   What are the men doing?

   In what are they interested?

   Which man shows great strength?

6. Who is the artist?

   Where is her great picture,—

   "The Horse Fair?"

Related Music: FESTIVAL AT BAG-DAD-RIMSKY—

   Last Half ....*Korsakow*

   THE WILD HORSEMAN

   ....*Schumann*

BEHIND THE PLOW
Private Collection

ARTIST: Lucy Kemp-Welch
SCHOOL: English
DATES: 1869-1958

BEHIND THE PLOW

Here is a farm by the seaside! The cool breezes blow in over the land. The white gulls circle in from the sea. They make a pretty pattern against the warm red of the plowed earth.

See the plow horses! They are, indeed, a pretty pair! One is dark and the other is light.

See the curves of their backs! The artist put the dark horse against the light sky so that the fine curves of his back could be seen. She put the white horse against the dark one, so that the curve of his back would be clearly outlined.

An artist thinks very carefully about placing the "lights" and "darks" in a picture. If the two horses should change places, do you think it would change the picture?

It is a very gentle breeze that blows in from the sea.

How the horses' tails are blowing back! They follow the long lines leading to the plow. The farmer lad guides the old-fashioned plow. He is turning up the rich red earth in the deep furrows.

See the red earth! Red is a very warm color. The unplowed field is a warm yellow. There is much warm color in the foreground of the picture.

Can you tell why the artist made a cool sea, off in the distance?

Can you tell why she suggested a breeze blowing in from the sea? Yes, yes, the cool blue water and the breeze from the sea cool off the warm red and yellow field. Warm colors and cool colors used together make a pleasing balance of color.

See, too, that the artist has repeated many colors in her picture.

The color of the dark horse is repeated in the warm red earth color. The white of the near horse is repeated in the clouds, the man's shirt, his hat, and the white sea gulls. White is a summer color. White is always cool.

An artist repeats his colors over a picture because it helps to draw them together into one design.

Do you see how the hard deep furrows lead the eye to the most important part of the picture, the "center of interest"? Yes, we follow the furrow along with the man and the plow, up to the fine pair of plow horses silhouetted against the sky.

Do you notice how the horses and the furrow lead off to the right? Do you notice how the farmer, the plow, and the sea gulls lead off to the left? Again, a little pull to the right, a little pull to the left, helps to make a well balanced picture.

Oh, there are so many things to think about when one paints a picture.

When the artist painted this picture she thought carefully about the warm colors and the cool colors, the balance to right and left, and the "center of interest." Because this has been so well done, her picture is beautiful. It is a work of art.

THE ARTIST

A few years ago the people of England made a great discovery. They found a young girl who was painting wonderful pictures of horses.

"Why!" they exclaimed, "this is an English Rosa Bonheur!" And it proved to be true.

Lucy Kemp-Welch is the Rosa Bonheur of England. She, too, loves to picture the "shiny coats" and the "rapid motion" of her beloved horses.

As a little girl living in a small village she saw no great exhibitions of pictures. She knew little about art and artists. It was a great day when the first picture exhibit came to her little town. Lucy stood before the paintings in admiring wonder.

By and by as she grew older she read the story of Rosa Bonheur. She learned how this little French girl became a celebrated painter of animals. It was thrilling to think that this great painter had once been a little girl like herself. She read the story of Landseer, too. He also was a great painter of animals. He became her hero. She had little prints of many famous pictures by these two artists. She studied them over and over.

At school her drawings were always considered very wonderful. After the regular lessons were finished, the teacher permitted the pupils to draw and paint anything they wished. Of course Lucy always gave attention to her studies. Then she found time to devote to drawing and painting.

As she became older she was delighted when told that she could go to art school. Here she applied herself to study. It was only for a short time, however, for she soon left the school to study by herself. Save for this short time in the art school Lucy Kemp-Welch was self-taught.

Day after day she drew and studied horses in all positions. No one paid any attention to the young English girl as she worked steadily along by herself.

But one day she sent a picture to the exhibition. It was a large painting called "To Arms." It was filled with men and animals in all sorts of difficult positions.

Immediately people began to ask about the picture and who the artist might be. Everybody marvelled. Everybody wondered who this Lucy Kemp-Welch could be.

By and by she exhibited more pictures. She began to receive added honors. Soon she was winning fame as a painter of animals.

Today Lucy Kemp-Welch lives in England. Back of her house is a great glass studio. It has very large glass doors which open out into an orchard. Here is an abundance of coarse grass and many picturesque trees which she finds useful in composing her pictures. In fine weather the artist poses the animals in the orchard. During the winter the horses are brought into the heated studio, which has a floor of earth. Here it is warm and comfortable. The artist has great love for these animals and makes every provision for their comfort. The horses seem to understand the artist and respond to her every word.

Here at her home her friends often look in at the great glass-covered room. Many times they find two plow horses, such as these in our picture, standing quietly in the midst of the studio, while off at one side the artist is busy at work.

Like Rosa Bonheur she likes to go among the horses to study them. It is said that she frequently visits a large hospital in England where she may study first hand. Nearly all her pictures are paintings of fine sturdy horses, such as those in our picture, "Behind the Plow."

DIRECTED STUDY

1. What is the season of the year?
   What kind of day is pictured?
   From what direction does the
      breeze blow?

2. Why is the dark horse placed
      against the sky?
   How is the white horse placed?
      Why?
   What would be the effect if
      they changed places?

3. How do the furrows run?
   How do the horses pull?
   How does the plowman lean? Why?
   How do the gulls circle? Why?

4. Name the warm colors.
   Name the cool colors.

5. What is the "center of inter-
      est?" How do you know?
   How is it emphasized?
   Give three points that help to
      make the picture a work of art.

6. Who is the artist? Where does
      she live?
   Do you like the picture? Why?

Related Music: PLOWING SONG . . . . .
                 . . . .*Chadwick*

VENETIAN WATERS
Budapest Museum

ARTIST: Ettore Tito
SCHOOL: Italian
DATES: 1859-1941

VENETIAN WATERS

Who wants to take a ride upon these shining waters?

Who will trust the sturdy gondolier?

What a wide stretch of water it is! It leads far out to sea.

How the sun sparkles on the water! See the many colors!

In the foreground the waves are big and strong. They lead out to sea, then turn and swing off to the left. They make long thin lines of yellow light. As they reach the horizon, the color fades into a smooth, calm, purple haze.

Perhaps the artist caught sight of this pretty scene as he walked by the water's edge. These sturdy Venetians, pushing their boats through the sparkling waters, made a pretty picture.

The artist began to draw. He placed the skyline high. This gives a far, far stretch of water. Then he began to swing wide-curving lines down to the very front of the picture. Next he added the boats, the pile, and the tiny sails afar.

The big dark boat, in the foreground, is tipped. The gondolier stands, barefoot, upon the stern. With rolled sleeves and tilted hat he plies his oar!

See how the sun has burned his skin! See how it shines on his leg, his arms, and his face!

He is a trusty gondolier! He knows how to balance himself on the moving boat! The little fellow in the front watches the artist as he works.

The man in the second boat is an

old hand at sea. He stands with safety on the far edge of his boat.

The orange-colored sails of the Venetian boat add a pretty bright color to the scene. Venetian sails are always gay!

See the reflections rippling in the water! They make a gay track of color down to the dark red blouse of the boy.

With so many colors, so many boats, and so many figures, can you find the "center of interest"?

Yes, to be sure! The big dark boat, and the gondolier plying his oar!

See how his oar and that of the second man repeat the slant of the sail. See how the curve of his strong shoulder and back swings in with the long curving lines of the waves as they near the boat. These same waves, swinging out to sea, would carry us out of the picture were it not for that little bright track of reflections under the Venetian boat. Instead of going out of the picture, we turn and come down this gay little path. It leads right into the big boat, and up to the trusty gondolier.

This is the way an artist emphasizes the most important part of a picture. The most important part of any picture is called, the "center of interest."

In our picture the artist made all the principal lines, the waves, and shadows lead to the center of interest, —the big boat, and the sturdy gondolier pushing his way through the sparkling waters of Venice.

THE ARTIST

We are not surprised that the artist who painted "Venetian Waters" lived in Venice. Only one who has lived beside the lazy lagoons, who has listened to the low song of the gondoliers, and who has watched the setting sun paint the waters of the Grand Canal, can make pictures of Venice. Such a one is Ettore Tito.

Tito was born in southern Italy in 1860. As a little boy he showed great promise along artistic lines. When he was twelve, he could draw and paint with some degree of skill. His parents were pleased by these signs of talent in their little son. They decided that his talent must be developed.

They lived not far from the city of

Venice. This city had been the home of many of the great artists of the past. They loved Venice because there they found beautiful color and sparkling light for their pictures.

Venice is a city of many little islands and all her streets are water. Here and there through the canals glide the many little gondolas. Never a horse, a wagon, or a car is seen in Venice! Everywhere is gay color and sparkling sunlight!

Here it was that the parents of the little Italian boy decided to send their son. Here he could have lessons in drawing and painting. Here he could see the great pictures of the world. Here, too, he would be living in one of the most picturesque cities in all the world, a city of bright sunlight.

Accordingly the lad went to Venice and began his studies. So delighted was he with his new school, so delighted was he with his work, that he gave all his time to study.

He soon made great progress, surprising both the teachers and students with his skill in drawing and his use of the color. Before long he was painting the pretty lagoons, the sparkling waters, and the gay gondolas of Venice.

When he was twenty-three years old he sent one of his pictures to a great exhibition in Rome. It attracted much attention. People began to praise his work. Soon he was made a teacher in the school where so many years before he had come to study.

Today Ettore Tito is the most famous living painter in Italy. It is his pictures of Italian life that have made him famous. Little fisherboys, in their old fishing boats, paintings of the sea, and the picturesque canals of Venice are his favorite subjects. These paintings, aglow with the light and color of Venice, are pictures of real life such as one sees every day in this city by the sea.

In all his pictures his figures are very natural. They look like real people. They act, too, like real people act. In our painting, "Venetian Waters," we see a real gondola of Venice. We see this sturdy gondolier expressing the action of handling the oar and pushing the boat through the water just as does the gondolier of Venice. The little boy standing in the front of the boat looks like hundreds of other little Italian boys who play around the wharf in Venice. The pose of the distant figure, standing on the far edge of the boat, is seen every day in this city by the sea. The gay colored sail of the Venetian boat is only one of many that lie at anchor along the Grand Canal. So it is with all the paintings of the artist. It is his picturing of real life, the natural- ness of his figures, and the excellent drawing of form and movement that have made him famous.

Not only is he the most famous artist in Italy, but he is one of the great artists of the world today.

DIRECTED STUDY

1. Where is this pretty scene?
   What time of year is it?
   What time of day is it?
   Where is the sun?

2. Why did the artist place the skyline high?
   What is the difference between the "near" waves and the "far waves"?
   What makes the color on the water."

3. What kind of lines do the waves make?
   Do they carry us out of the picture?

4. Where is the sunlight brightest?
   Describe the sturdy gondolier.

5. Where is the "center of inter-
      est?"
   How is it emphasized?

6. Who is the artist?
   What kind of pictures
      does he paint?
   What is his nationality?
   Do you like the picture? Why?

Related Music: GONDOLIER ..... *Nevin*
                 BARCAROLLE—
                 Tales of Hoffman
                   ....*Offenbach*

THE SHEEPFOLD
Hermitage, St. Petersburg

ARTIST: Charles-Émile Jacque
SCHOOL: French
DATES: 1813-1894

THE SHEEPFOLD

How warm and comfortable this sheepfold! It may be cold and wintry without, but within all is warmth, peace, and contentment.

A sheepfold such as this is very commonly seen in the country districts of France. You will be surprised to learn that this artist, Charles Émile Jacque, kept a sheepfold on his little farm just for the sake of study. He kept many sheep. He also kept chickens and pigs. He was a lover of all these farmyard animals. With his pencil, brush, and paints he continually studied the woolly sheep, the lambs, the lumbering pigs, and the gay roosters of his poultry yard.

In our picture he looks within the

sheepfold. There he sees a bright glow lighting up the floor and the wall. He sees the bright light shining in at the two little windows. All the rest of the fold is in deep shadow. This made a beautiful pattern of "dark" and "light."

See the long line of the manger against the left wall! It leads back to the far end of the fold. It is filled with fresh hay. Here the sheep may nibble at ease. The long lines of the roof-beams follow the same direction, leading back to the end wall. These are rough tree timber, but they doubtless support a well thatched roof. On the opposite wall are the two little windows with the warm sunlight streaming in.

See the center of the fold! See the

golden straw! The shepherd stands at the swinging manger, busy and intent on his work. His blue shirt makes a spot of pretty color in the light, and his hat turns gold.

All around are the sheep. Some stand nibbling at the straw in the swinging manger. Others are walking about. One large sheep lies with his woolly back in the full light.

Two little white lambs make two light spots in the picture. Do you see how the artist has placed them? They stand on the edge of the lighted path that leads right up to the shepherd! This was the artist's plan! This is the way he leads into his picture, to the "center of interest."

On the opposite side, on the dark

edge of the path, is a large basket, and beside it a little red rooster. Jacque always likes his gay-colored poultry about!

Do you see that the color of the fold is a deep warm earth color? Do you see that there are three spots of red in the picture? The large rack on the right takes on a deep rich red. Opposite, on the wall, hangs an object of similar hue. Next, the little red rooster in the front of the picture completes the trio. These three spots of red keep us within the fold just as the artist intended!

It is the *way* he arranged his color and the *way* he planned the dark and light parts of his picture into a pattern, that have made this artist famous.

THE STORY OF THE ARTIST

This painter has a long French name. Do you think you can pronounce it, Charles Émile Jacque?

Charles Émile Jacque was a painter of sheep, pigs, and poultry. He raised sheep, pigs, and poultry on his little farm in France. He lived on this little farm so he could always be near them. Here he studied them as much as he liked.

He lived near another great French painter. This was Millet. Both artists painted peasants. Jacque, however, became famous for his paintings of sheep, pigs, and poultry, while Millet was called "the painter of peasants."

He and Millet were very good friends. They often spent the long evenings together, talking about their pictures and their many ideas in art.

Jacque was not only a painter, but he was a successful business man as well. Everything he touched turned to gold! He was a man of great energy and force, and every business venture was a success.

At one time he bought many pictures of other artists, kept them for a time, and then sold them at a handsome profit. This business he carried on for years.

He bought houses and lands. He painted pictures, and occasionally wrote a book. He once wrote a book on the history of the hen, and illustrated it with his own drawings. His special hobby, however, was his sheep, pigs, and poultry. His picturing of these barnyard animals was remarkable. The paintings for which he has become famous are largely of sheep, going to pasture, grazing, returning at even, or secure in the sheepfold.

Though his pictures are small, they are always painted in a big, bold way. Fortunately the artist lived to see his work appreciated. He received many, many medals and honors during the latter part of his life.

His mind was a great storehouse of art knowledge, and of the interesting experiences of a lifetime. In later years after he had grown to be an old man, he entertained his friends with stories of his life. He used to laugh about his many experiences in business. He talked about his pictures. He talked about his farmyard animals, his sheep, pigs, and poultry. But he liked best of all to tell about his many interesting visits with his great and good friend, Millet.

DIRECTED STUDY

1. What is a sheepfold?
   What is the season of the year?
   How do you know?

2. From what direction does the
     light come?
   Where does it shine brightest?
   Where does it lead the eye?
   What is this part of a picture
     called?
   Why is it important?

3. What is the farmer doing?
   Are all the sheep doing the
      same thing?
   Do the little lambs add to the
      picture? How?

4. Name other objects you see
      in the fold.

5. What is the color of the interior?
   Why did the artist make it this
      color?
   Do you see any cool color?

6. Who is the artist?
   What did he like best to paint?

Related Music: INTERMEZZO—
                CAVALLIERA RUSTI-
                CANO ....*Mascagni*

THE GLEANERS
Louvre, Paris

ARTIST: Jean-François Millet
SCHOOL: French
DATES: 1814-1875

THE GLEANERS

What a busy day! Harvest time is the busiest time of all the year!

Boys and girls who live in the cities know little about farm life, and the grand and glorious days of harvest time! They never see the great fields of golden grain unless perchance they visit in the country.

The wheat fields of America are much like those of other countries.

This picture shows a wheat field in France. The whole scene is aglow with the sun high up in the sky.

See how high the artist has placed the skyline! This gives a vast stretch of field. The harvesting has been completed, and now the men are building great stacks of golden grain. Some are binding the wheat into sheaves. Others are pitching it into a high wagon.

Just see the high stacks! Just see the busy workers! The overseer sits on his horse directing the work. His fleet steed carries him swiftly from one part of the field to another. Thus he keeps all his men busy through the long day.

The women, too, are busy. After the wheat has been harvested, they are sent out to pick up the scattered stalks and heads of grain. Here the three strong women are gleaning the remnants of the crop. They are called "gleaners."

Two of the women have turned up their aprons to form a kind of sack or bag to hold the grain. Bent over they swing along, carrying the grain from the ground to the apron, or throwing the long stalks to the other hand.

Notice the "far" woman. She picks up the long straws and swings them over her shoulder to the hand resting, palm up, on her back. The others have the long stalks in their aprons.

The whole field glows with the warm summer sun. Only the dress of the women takes on different hues. Like all peasants they wear their hair bound in a soft cloth. They have pulled down the edge to shade the eyes. Their clothes are dark in color and of coarse material.

Notice the way the artist has placed the three women. They are not in a row, neither are they close together.

He placed the two "far" women side by side. He placed the "near" one a little apart. This makes the group more interesting.

The artist wanted us to see the three peasant women first, so he drew them large and gave them the most important place in the picture. He also wanted us to see the grain stacks and the far reaching field, so he curved the back of the "near" woman. With your pencil, trace up along the curved back. It carries straight to the distant stacks!

This is the way an artist leads from one part of his picture to another. This is the way he takes the eye all over the picture at a glance. This is the way he makes *one* picture of many figures.

THE ARTIST

The artist who painted "The Gleaners" was himself a hard-working peasant. Jean François Millet knew all about the never-ending labor of the French farm. As a little boy he had worked in the fields. In his spare time he had made many sketches of the sheep as they grazed in the meadow. One day he modeled them in some soft clay he had found on the farm. By and by he sketched and modeled the figures of peasants as he watched them at work in the fields.

The people all said that he would be an artist. His father, too, said that his little son must have lessons in drawing. It was his dear old grandmother, however, who understood best that little Jean had great talent. She it was who had always taken gentle care of the little boy. From the time he had been a baby she had rocked him to sleep. She had told him many, many stories. Most of all she had told him stories from the Bible.

The first pictures that Jean had seen were those in his grandmother's Bible. He used to sit by the hour and copy these pictures. His grandmother was very happy when she saw him so busy at this work. More pleased, however, was she when she saw the wonderful little drawings he had made. Then and there she decided that the child must have proper instruction in drawing.

Finally his father resolved to send

him to a neighboring city for study. Once there, however, the people were so astonished at his skill that no one had the courage to teach him. Then he went to the great city of Paris to study.

Paris had always been a dream city to the little artist. Now he was really in the great art center of the world!

He walked through the beautiful art gallery looking at the wonderful pictures. Little did he dream that some day his own pictures would be among the greatest to hang in this same gallery!

Millet worked long and hard, but he had little success in selling his pictures. As he grew older he painted pictures of the peasants of France at their daily labor. Sometimes it was the hard worker in the field. Sometimes it was the worker in the home. Always, however, it was the French peasant at his daily toil.

But the public did not care for pictures of working people, and would not buy. Poor Millet was without money and often without food. This, however, did not entirely discourage him. He still kept on with his work.

One day he painted his picture of "The Gleaners." When he exhibited it a storm of disapproval arose. It pictured women working in the fields, and the public did not like it. They did not like to be reminded of the hard work that the French peasant women had to do. But Millet was not trying to make "pretty" pictures. Instead he pictured the truth as he saw it about him. This was the busy toilsome life of the country people. He pictured their humility, their patience, and faithfulness in face of the constant drudgery which was their lot.

Though the people were very indignant because Millet had painted this picture of working women, it was finally sold for $400. This seemed a large sum to Millet. Later, however, it was sold again, and this time for $60,000, and the condition was added that some day it should be given to the famous picture gallery in Paris.

Today this picture is one of the treasures of this same gallery that

Millet visited so often when he first came to the great city. Today a Millet picture brings a fabulous price and Millet is recognized as one of the great artists of the world.

DIRECTED STUDY

1. What is the setting of the
      picture?
   What proportion is field?
      Sky?
   How does the artist give
      distance?

2. What does it mean to "glean?"
   What are the three women doing?
   Are they contented? Thrifty?
   How are they dressed?

3. What is the time of year?
   What is the time of day?

4. What is going on in the background?
   What does the rider do?

5. Where is the "center of interest?" How do you know?
   How is it emphasized?
   How has the artist carried us
   back into the picture?

6. Who is the artist?
   What kind of pictures did he
   paint?
   How were his pictures received?
   How are they regarded today?

Related Music: —CHANSON TRISTE
   .... *Tschaikowsky*

   FIFTH SYMPHONY—
   Andante .... *Beethoven*

THE SOLEMN PLEDGE
Art Institute, Chicago

ARTIST: Walter Ufer
SCHOOL: American
DATES: 1876-1936

THE SOLEMN PLEDGE

See the fine dark heads of the Indians! They are very solemn! Something unusual is taking place. They are looking at the youth who stands at the left.

See the stern face of the tallest Indian! See him as he eyes the young boy! The next Indian looks very grave, and is deeply interested in the lad. His friend below lays a hand upon his arm, and looks earnestly into his face.

There stands the young Indian boy! He is very serious. He is making a solemn promise. He is making a pledge of friendship. It is, indeed, a solemn pledge.

This artist says that in his country

the Indians often have misunderstandings. Sometimes one Indian will be hostile to another. Then one of the elders tries to bring about a friendly feeling. Sometimes they go to the fields to make the pledge of friendship. Sometimes they go up into the hills.

Many times a little pile of stones is raised to commemorate the solemn pledge which each has taken. Sometimes this monument is made by the friends of each side, in turn, laying in stones until quite a pile is raised. All through the State of New Mexico these little piles of stones are seen. They tell of a solemn pledge of friendship made sometime in the past.

Here stand the Indians in the great out-of-doors. The open country lies all about them.

See the sage-brush of the desert! See the distant dark mountain! See the cloud forms above!

How rugged, and stern, and strong they are! They are just like the figures of the Indians.

See how the artist has grouped his figures! They stand very close, in a compact mass. See the pattern they make against the background!

They wear the great white blankets of their tribe. See the broad, simple surface of the blankets! How they emphasize the dark heads of the Indians!

The standing youth wears a blanket, too. It has dropped to his waist. We see the warm yellow shirt that he wears.

See his fine dark head! See the long braids as they fall over his shoulders! See the little line of light about his head! The light must shine full upon his face, too, although we cannot see it.

This is the land of brilliant, dazzling light!

All the light in the picture is made by the artist's color. He knew just how to choose his color. He knew just how to place his color.

How the light plays along the edges of the other figures! It lights up the shoulders of the tallest Indian. It touches his thick coarse hair with light. See it as it shines on the dark copper color of his skin!

It also plays along the outline of the second Indian. Below it falls full upon the face of the young boy. It touches the top of his dark hair, too.

See how it lights up the shoulders of the yellow shirt! Yes, light is everywhere! The bright, clear sunlight of Taos!

It is the painting of light, and the strong pattern or design of his pictures that has brought fame to this artist.

"The Solemn Pledge" is one of the prize pictures of the artist. It now hangs in the permanent collection of the Art Institute of Chicago.

THE STORY OF THE ARTIST

The artist who painted this picture lives in Taos, New Mexico, the land of the Pueblo Indian. His name is Walter Ufer. He is one of the foremost modern artists of America. Today many American artists are making their homes in this western land.

Taos is a sage-brush desert seven thousand feet above sea level. Around it rises the giant mountains to a height of thirteen thousand feet. Here is a sky that is always blue. Here is a sun that is always shining. Here is color everywhere!

And then the Indians! These superb copper-colored fellows wrapped in their white blankets are a marked contrast to the "pale-faces" who come from the East. Over seven hundred of the finest Indians in America live in Taos. No wonder the artists are making their homes in this western country!

Though Mr. Ufer lives in the west he was born in Louisville, Kentucky. There he went to school just like other little boys. There his teacher learned that he liked to draw. She found him making sketches on the pages of his reader. The principal, too, found that the little Walter had great talent. One day he asked him what he wanted to be when he grew to be a man. "An artist," immediately replied the little fellow.

So determined was he to become a

painter that he planned, when still a child to earn money for study. He did many kinds of work. Like so many ambitious American boys of today, he carried a paper route. Rain or shine, through all kinds of weather, on he trudged.

By taking care of the pennies, earned on the paper route, and adding to them little by little, he managed to save a small bank account. This he planned to use for his studies.

When he was a young lad he went to the World's Fair in Chicago. Here he saw the great White City with its beautiful walks, buildings, pictures, and sculpture. The exhibition of pictures interested him most.

He wanted more than ever to be a

painter! It was his one desire.

By and by opportunities came to him. He studied both in America and Europe. He won many honors.

When he returned to America in 1914, he went to this western land of the Pueblo Indian, a land of light and color. Here he painted many of his famous pictures.

For many years Walter Ufer has continued to carry off many prizes and honors. All his pictures make one feel the bigness and grandeur of the West.

Instead of painting landscape and figures just as they are, he weaves them into beautiful patterns or designs. Such a pattern is our picture, "The Solemn Pledge."

Within recent years many new honors have come to the artist. His pictures now hang in many of the important galleries of America.

Mr. Ufer says he *won* his success. And more, "One can win only through hard work."

DIRECTED STUDY

1. Where do these Indians live?
   To what tribe do they belong?
   Can you name other tribes
     in America?

2. What kind of country is this?
   What kind of day?
   What color is used most
     in the picture? Why?
   Where is the sun? How do you
     know?

3. How does the sun fall upon the
   tallest Indian? On the seated
   boy? On the standing boy?
   Where is the darkest part of
   of the pattern?

4. Do the clouds add to the picture? How?
   Does the mountain add to the
   picture? How?

5. Who is the artist?
   For what is he especially known?

6. Where does the picture hang?

Related Music: THE SACRIFICE
             (*Indian Mourning Song*)

PREPARING FOR CHURCH
Private Collection

ARTIST: Bernandus J. Blommers
SCHOOL: Dutch
DATES: 1845-1914

PREPARING FOR CHURCH

It is Sunday in Holland. Sunday is a happy day for the Holland peasant. On this day he forgets his work-a-day clothes. He forgets his comfortable wooden shoes. Dressed in his very best, with Bible in hand, he wends his way over the fields or along the lazy canals to the village church. This is his first duty. This is his first pleasure.

See the shy peasant girl! She will not let us see her pretty face unless we look into the mirror. There, she is smiling at us!

The peasant lad sits patiently waiting. A mischievous light twinkles in his eye. Soon that unruly curl will be arranged! Then off together they will go to the village church.

See the pretty room! It is a room in a typical Dutch house. The light coming in from a window gives it a gay glad color.

See the old red chest! Nearly everything in the room catches the light of this gay red chest. It tints the dress and apron of the Dutch maid. Its gay color is reflected in the lad's dark clothes. We see it again in the mirror frame, and in the mirror, too! It tints up the floor and the walls. Red is everywhere, except, perhaps, in the green curtain. The artist keeps the curtain green because red and green make a pleasing contrast of hue. One is a warm color, the other cool. Warm and cool colors always help to make a beautiful picture.

On the chest sits a model of a Holland boat. This is just such a boat as the Hollander loves. He has always lived where the North Sea skirts the coast. From his childhood he has seen these great masted schooners lying along the wharf.

About the wall runs the deep tile wainscoting. Nearly all Dutch rooms have pretty tiles about the wall, for tiles are made in Holland.

The artist has placed two little straight backed chairs in the room. The young lad sits beside the red chest. He looks fine in his Sunday clothes! His wooden shoes have been exchanged for those that are low and comfortable. See the great rosettes on the instep! He holds in his hand the little Bible, with its dainty clasp. On the floor rests his Sunday hat.

The Dutch maiden, too, is in her best dress. She wears the typical full skirt, a violet apron, and the little white cap. Her jacket hangs upon the corner chair. She, too, wears her dainty Sunday slippers.

The light from the window falls full upon her. It lights her pretty blouse, her violet apron, and light red dress. The light falls upon the lad's clothes, too, but they remain the darkest note in the picture. Here, about the red chest, the artist has placed his strongest color and his sharpest contrasts. Here he holds our attention. Here is the "center of interest."

The artist wanted us to see not only the "center of interest," but all over the picture as well. So he placed certain accents on the floor below, and on the wall above. The boy's hat carries a dark accent to the lower part of the picture, while the mirror adds another above. The hat, the lad, and maid, and the happy face in the mirror make our picture.

Though we see all over the painting, though we like the Dutch room with its pretty tiles and its gay contrast of red and green, we always come back to the happy face of the peasant lad, and the shy winsome smile in the mirror.

Soon that unruly curl will be arranged! Then she with her jacket and he with his tall Sunday hat will be off for the village church.

THE ARTIST

Two hundred years ago the artists of Holland found their greatest pleasure in painting little pictures of every day life. Pretty little rooms where the sunlight trickles in, or where a soft daylight spreads over walls and floor are the pictures which have brought fame to Holland.

Two hundred years ago the greatest artists of Holland were painting just such little scenes. They were called "little Dutchmen" because their pictures were very small. They were only large enough to hang on the walls of the simple homes of the Hollanders.

Today, after all these years, the artists of Holland are again painting these same little interiors, aglow with light.

Bernandus J. Blommers is one of these modern painters. His pictures usually tell a story of the simple life of the Dutch peasants.

When this painter was a little fellow, he liked best to draw and paint. His father, however, wanted him to grow up and become a business man. But the young lad had no thoughts of business. He spent all his leisure time in drawing and painting the people about him.

Later, as he grew older, people began to praise his work. This gave him great joy.

After many years he became known as one of the foremost painters of Holland. Nearly all his paintings picture the happy Dutch peasants and their cottage interiors.

DIRECTED STUDY

1. From what country comes this pretty scene?
   What is an interior?
   How much of this picture is floor? Wall?

2. Why is the mirror placed on the wall?
   Why is the curtain at the left?

3. From what direction comes the
      light?
   What is the dominant color?
   Where is it repeated?
   Do you like the green curtains?
   Why?

4. Describe the dress of the maid.
      Of the lad.
   Are they happy?

5. What is the "center of interest"?
   How is it accented?

6. Who is the artist?
   What kind of pictures does he
      paint?
   Do you like this picture? Why?

Related Music: CAVATINA .... *Roff*

GOING TO MARKET
Hermitage, St. Petersburg

ARTIST: Constant Troyon
SCHOOL: French
DATES: 1810-1865

GOING TO MARKET

Early misty morning finds many French farmers on their way to market. It is a long, long road from the farm to the market, and the patient cows and sheep never hurry.

The two women of our picture have risen early. With their sheep, cows, and vegetables they have started on the long road to town.

The morning still slumbers. All is quiet and still. Only the muffled patter of little feet, and the occasional bark of a playful dog is heard. The drowsy trees are bathed in the misty atmosphere of dawn. The early morning light sends a soft glow down the long road. It lights up the backs of the woolly sheep. It lights up the backs of the cows. It lays long shadows on the narrow country road.

See the gray hazy sky of early morning! See the misty edges of the trees! See the long shadows! By and by, as the sun rises, the shadows will become shorter and shorter. The trees will awaken. The sky will be aglow with the light of day.

In the midst of the group comes the patient little donkey, laden with baskets of produce. Such a little fellow! Such a big load! And there on his back sits the little farmer woman. She will have a long ride to market! The older woman follows, keeping a watchful eye on the flock.

See the figures of the two women!

See the silhouettes they make against the morning sky. The "far" woman is gray in the distance. The "near" woman is in dark red color. The artist thinks this is the most important part of his picture!

See the curved branch of the tree at the left. It curves like the peasant woman's back. It curves down to the light woolly backs of the sheep.

On the other side are the cows, The light shines here also. It shines brightest on the big basket. Here the artist has placed the light basket next the dark red color of the peasant woman's dress. This makes a sharp contrast. A sharp contrast helps to make the most important part of a picture. So in our picture, the little peasant woman sitting on the donkey is the "center of interest." The light all about her makes the edges of her dark figure very clear against the early morning sky. Thus, you see, the artist thought very carefully about the pattern of "dark" and "light" in his picture.

Have you noticed that the artist has only drawn two or three sheep?

Of course you know there are many more!

Look closely. You will find that you really do not see the sheep. You see only the light play over their rounded woolly backs.

See the soft hazy coloring of red and green! Each hue is repeated again and again in many different tones. The dark rich red of the peasant woman is repeated in the cows, the light color of the little roof, and the still lighter glow in the road. The green changing into grays is repeated in grass, house, and distant trees.

It is by repeating his color again and again over his picture that the artist makes his color-pattern. An artist always gives much thought to placing his colors in the color-pattern.

Although this artist is first of all an animal painter, he liked to paint the early morning just as it appeared, with its mysterious light and shadow, and the forms of his beloved cattle silhouetted against it.

THE ARTIST

As a painter of animals Constant Troyon divided honors with Rosa Bonheur. It is almost impossible to believe that this painter of sturdy cows and sheep was first a painter upon china.

Constant Troyon was born near the great porcelain factory of Sevres, France, in 1810. His father and grandfather before him had worked there as decorators of china. It was only natural that the boy, too, should grow up within its walls.

Troyon's father died when he was a small boy of seven, leaving the mother to care for her two little sons. The great porcelain factory was only a short distance from the home. Here many men and boys from the surrounding country were employed to add the decoration to the fine china. It is not surprising that the mother looked to the porcelain factory as a source of income for herself and her two small sons.

As soon as the lad was old enough he went to work in the factory. Here he had his first lessons in art. Here he drew and painted the pretty designs upon china.

He worked day by day but all the time he wanted to paint pictures. Pictures of the fields and trees, of the green grass and blue skies of France were the subjects he wanted to paint.

One day he went out into the fields. He carried a large canvas with him.

This he covered with a scene direct from nature. Troyon painted, first of all for his own pleasure, so he did not care about selling his pictures. When his friends, however, saw the large canvases filled with these familiar scenes they urged him to send them to the exhibition. At first he hesitated. Finally, however, he yielded to the wishes of his friends and sent his pictures to be exhibited.

To his great surprise he was overwhelmed with praise. He became very popular. People liked his pictures because they were truthful representations of nature. This gave him new encouragement. He resolved to give all his time to painting. He resolved to become an artist.

One day he went to Holland. There he saw the great expanse of sky, the level lowlands, and the sturdy breeds of Holland cattle. These grand creatures decided his course. He resolved to become a painter of animals.

From that time on he gave his attention to the painting and drawing of sheep and cattle. Usually he placed his cows and sheep in beautiful landscape settings of early morning, high noon, or late evening. Sometimes the forms of the cattle are silhouetted against a morning light. Sometimes they appear in finished perfection in the full light of day.

Troyon is a peer among the animal painters of the world. During his lifetime he received many honors. His pictures were as famous in England and Holland as they were in his own country.

Today his pictures hang in the greatest galleries of the world. Many of his choice paintings have found their way to America.

DIRECTED STUDY

1. What is the time of day?
   How do you know?
   Describe the atmosphere. The
      trees.

2. Where is the little group going?
   What direction do they travel?
   How can you tell?

3. From what direction comes the
   light?
   Where does it fall?

4. How do the forms of the animals
   appear? Of the women? Why?
   What makes the long shadows?

5. Name the two principal colors
   in the picture.
   Where is each repeated?
   Where is the strongest color?
   The brightest light? Why?

6. Who is the painter?
   What decided him to become an
   animal painter?
   Name other animal painters.

Related Music: BEIGERE LEGERE—
                 Old French . . . .

THE BLUE BOY
Huntington Collection, Pasadena, California

ARTIST: Thomas Gainsborough
SCHOOL: English
DATES: 1727-1788

THE BLUE BOY

Over one hundred and fifty years ago there lived in England, a young lad of fifteen. His name was Jonathan Buttall. His father was very rich. He wished to have a portrait of his fine young son.

In that day pictures were not taken with a camera as they are today. Indeed, no one but an artist could make a portrait. So Jonathan's father sent for one of the greatest artists in England. This artist was Thomas Gainsborough.

Just about this time someone had said that it was impossible to paint a "blue" picture. Gainsborough thought much about this. He didn't quite believe it. He decided to paint a "blue" picture, and to make it as beautiful as any picture in the world. When he set out to paint the portrait of the young Master Jonathan, he decided that this should be his "blue" picture.

See the beautiful blue silk suit! The trousers are short and are tied with ribbons below the knee. The coat is short, too. It has slashed sleeves that show the dainty white blouse beneath. He wears a wonderful lace collar and cuffs. Lace collars and cuffs were so fashionable when Master Jonathan was a boy!

He wears silk stockings and slippers with ribbon bows. And what shall we say of his fine hat with the great white ostrich plume? Plumed hats were so fashionable when Master Jonathan was a boy!

Here he stands for his picture. His blue coat is thrown over one arm. His plumed hat is in his right hand. How straight he stands, this young Master Jonathan!

The light must fall from above, for it lights his face and part of his pretty blue suit.

See the pretty glints of light across the surface of the blue silk!

The artist put a warm gray sky behind the lad. Blue and gray are beautiful together. One is warm and the other is cool. He stands beside a little garden lake with green shrubs growing near. He makes a fine silhouette against the sky. His face is happy and contented as he watches the artist work. Master Jonathan knows he will have a fine picture!

Sure enough, when the portrait was finished it was pronounced a masterpiece. Gainsborough had proved that is is possible to make a picture beautiful, though painted in "blue."

Everybody called it the "Blue Boy." It has been called "The Blue Boy" ever since.

Today this beautiful picture hangs in a collection of paintings in America. Master Jonathan never dreamed that his portrait, painted so many years ago, would find a new home in a land so far away.

It was in the summer of 1921 that the people of England said good-by to the famous boy in blue. His picture was hung in a great gallery in London. For many days the people thronged the gallery for a last farewell.

There stood the handsome blue boy, his hat in hand, to greet them. He looked at the people as they passed. There were so many people. Many had tears in their eyes. They were sorry to see him go. He had lived in England so long, and now he was leaving forever.

Master Jonathan, too, was sorry to leave dear, old England. He looked at his host of friends. A shy smile played over his face. He seemed to say,—"Yes, yes, I am going away, but remember, it is only to our cousins across the sea."

THE STORY OF THE ARTIST

Thomas Gainsborough is one of the great painters of the world. He was born in England two hundred years ago.

It is said that when he was only six years old he could sketch rapidly, and at twelve he was a good painter

At school he covered his books with sketches. He was never so happy as when, with pencil in hand, he set out to make a sketch of some beautiful old hedge or bit of landscape.

One day he wanted to go sketching. He declared it was too beautiful to stay in-doors. He wrote a note to his teacher saying, "Give Tom a holiday," and signed his father's name.

When he reached home in the evening he told his father about the note. His father was inclined to scold, but when he saw Tom's sketches he changed his mind. He declared the boy was a genius.

Finally Tom's uncle advised that the boy be sent to London to study. Accordingly when he was about fifteen, young Gainsborough set out for London.

Here he remained many years. He was a serious-minded boy, and gave careful thought to his studies.

At first he painted landscapes. Later he began to paint portraits. Soon he became one of the great portrait painters of England.

He was a musician as well as a painter. He played upon many musical instruments. It has been said that he is an artist who "sings in color." This means that his colors have a life and freshness which make them vibrate like music. "The Blue Boy" is one of his most famous paintings.

DIRECTED STUDY

1. Who is this handsome boy?
   Where did he live? When?

2. Why did the artist paint
      a "blue" picture?
   How does a painting differ
      from a photograph?

3. Describe the boy's costume.
   Name the colors.
   Name the colors in the
      background.

4. Name the cool colors.
   Name the warm colors.

5. From what direction does the
      light come?
   Where does it fall?
   Why did the artist arrange
      the light in this way?

6. What do you like best about
      the portrait?
   Who is the artist?
   Why is it said that he
      "sings in color"?

Related Music: NARCISSUS ..... *Nevin*
                SYMPHONY (Unfinished)
                First Movement *Schubert*

PRONUNCIATION OF PROPER NAMES

BLOMMERS . . . . (blŏm′ ẽrs)

BONHEUR . . . . (bō′ nûr′)

JACQUE, CHARLES ÉMILE . .
. . . . (shärls ā′ mēl′ zhạwk)

MILLET, JEAN FRANÇOIS. . .
. . . . . . (zhän frön′ swä′ mē′ yā′)

PUEBLO . . . . (pwĕb′ lō)

RENI, GUIDO . . . (gwē′ dō rā′ nē)

TAOS . . . . (tous)

TITO, ETTORE . . (ăt tor′ ă tē′ tō)

TROYON . . . . (trwä′ yôn′)

UFER . . . . (ōō′ fẽr)

SUGGESTIONS TO TEACHERS

STUDYING THE PICTURE. Any picture presented for study becomes more interesting when freely discussed in a natural way by the class. Before reading the text it is always advisable to study the picture. Pupils should be encouraged to give their own impressions; tell what they like in a picture, and WHY they like it.

In the intermediate and grammar grades simple elements in picture making may be pointed out,—i.e. light and shade, repetition of line, of color, color harmony, balance, and center of interest. Such questions as,—From what direction does the light come? Where does it shine brightest?—and others of a similar nature, may help the pupil to SEE. Led by the teacher's skillful questioning, pupils gradually acquire the ability to discover for themselves many elements of design in picture-making.

DRAMATIZATION. Many of the pictures used in the intermediate and grammar grades lend themselves to dramatization. Under no circumstances is it necessary to burden one's self, in the class room, with an exact reproduction. The details of costume are not required. Any outstanding accessory of dress, easily at hand, may, however, add interest. It is the pose of the figure, the grouping if there are several, and the action, that are best appreciated by the pupils when the effort is made to reproduce a picture.

CORRELATION. Many of the famous pictures of this series bear directly upon interesting historical events. These, in particular, furnish subjects for language and composition.

Drawing lessons may with real profit be given over to the tracing of pictures, for the purpose of studying line, composition, light and shade.

The music hour offers still another opportunity for related study. Pictures, like music, create emotions. When possible in the study of pictures, add the music which suggests the spirit and atmosphere of the picture. THE INTEREST IS ALWAYS KEENLY STIMULATED WHEN PORTIONS FROM VARIOUS SELECTIONS ARE PLAYED, AND THE CHILDREN PERMITTED TO CHOOSE THE ONE BEST SUITED TO THE PICTURE.

The suggestions for musical renderings, selections which follow the questions on the picture, will be of great value to the teacher.

As far as possible, each pupil should own his own pictures. This leads to the making of picture-study books, envelopes, and folders, for preserving his pictures.

STUDY OF ARTISTS. Many times when studying an artist, children are delighted to bring to the class room other reproductions of his pictures. This always stimulates interest. With several pictures by the same artist before the class, the outstanding characteristics of the painter, whether in color, composition, or some other phase of picture-making, may be intelligently discussed by the pupils. After such study as this, what "Millet" or "Rembrandt" will not be instantly recognized!

Sometimes pictures of the same subject by different artists is an equally interesting form of study. Such a series under a general subject,—as "K n i g h t h o o d," "Trees," "Boats," "Joan of Arc,"—affords many opportunities for valuable comparisons. Children will readily discover that each of the artists, treating the same subject, tells his story in a different way. This cultivates intelligent SEEING, and appreciation.

Free discussion and pictures before the class are always vital to real enjoyment of the masterpieces.

To be introduced in early years to the masterpieces of the ages, and to learn of the kingly minds who have ruled in this realm of beauty, is sure to develop an interest which will enlarge, enrich, and refine the future life of the pupil.

www.ingramcontent.com/pod-product-compliance
Lightning Source LLC
Chambersburg PA
CBHW041718090426
42739CB00018B/3470